Immortal Diamond

The Spiritual Vision of
Gerard Manley Hopkins

Image Books
Doubleday
New York London Toronto Sydney Auckland

An Image Book

PUBLISHED BY DOUBLEDAY

a division of Bantam Doubleday Dell Publishing Group, Inc.
1540 Broadway, New York, New York 10036

Image, Doubleday, and the portrayal of a deer drinking from a
stream are trademarks of Doubleday, a division of Bantam
Doubleday Dell Publishing Group, Inc.

First Image Books edition published July 1995
by special arrangement with Doubleday.

Library of Congress Cataloging-in-Publication Data

Hopkins, Gerard Manley, 1844–1889.
Immortal diamond: the spiritual vision of
Gerard Manley Hopkins / Gerard Manley Hopkins.
— 1st Image books ed.
p.   cm.
"An Image book"—T.p. verso.
1. Christian poetry, English.   2. Spiritual life—Poetry.
I. Title.
PR4803.H44A6   1995a
821'.8—dc20   95-837
                                        CIP

ISBN 0-385-47846-1

Contents

Introduction

The posthumous publication of Gerard Manley Hopkins's poetry in 1918 did not at first arouse much interest in readers, but in subsequent years the work of this poet-priest has taken its place among the most beloved spiritual writings of all time. The profound mix of technical ability, rich imagery, and spiritual yearning found in his poetry has earned Hopkins distinction as one of the greatest writers ever to give voice to the experience of the divine.

Hopkins was born on July 28, 1844, into an Anglican family in Essex. He began writing poetry at a young age and already exhibited promise as a poet when he entered Oxford University at the age of nineteen. Because of his obvious talent and his strong affinity for nature, many were reminded of the young Keats. Over time at Oxford, though, he began to cultivate a more ascetic side, less concerned with reveling in his senses and more centered on a disciplined intellect. Toward the end of his

Oxford career he became increasingly influenced by Cardinal Newman, and eventually applied to Newman for entry into the Catholic Church.

During his ascetic investigations at Oxford he often considered dedicating his life to religion, but it was not until 1868 that he made the decision to enter the Jesuit novitiate and study for the priesthood. Wanting to begin his entrance to the Jesuit order with a clean break from the past, he burned all his poetry as a sacrifice to his new life, and he did not write any verse for several years. He did, however, continue to keep a journal, and entries from his first years as a Jesuit novice show how he reenergized his earlier love of nature and synthesized it with his more recently developed religious discipline.

He did return to the composition of poetry in 1875 when his rector encouraged him to write "The Wreck of the Deutschland." This was not an easy step for him, however, and for the rest of his life he would wrestle with the question of whether he could in good conscience dedicate any portion of his life to poetry. In him there was a strong awareness that pride and the quest for fame were incompatible with the spiritual life he wanted to lead.

After his ordination into the priesthood in 1877, he went on to perform parish work in England, later taking teaching positions in both England and, later, Ireland. It is during this period that he wrote the majority of the poems. He died in Dublin on June 8, 1889.

Today, Gerard Manley Hopkins is recognized as one of the fathers of modern poetry. Far from being regarded as representative of the Victorian era in which he lived, his remarkably inventive technique is seen by many as being even more progressive than that of many modern poets. This is most apparent in his desire to use language that is close to actual spoken speech, language that is authentic (or natural) in style and meter.

As important as his technical ability, though, is the unique quality of spiritual wonder that runs through all his work. Readers today will feel deep resonance with these timeless expressions of the divine, and will marvel at the ability of a human who was able to put into words what had always seemed to belong to the realm of the inexpressible.

The Alchemist
in the City

My window shows the travelling clouds,
Leaves spent, new seasons, alter'd sky,
The making and the melting crowds:
The whole world passes; I stand by.

They do not waste their meted hours,
But men and masters plan and build:
I see the crowning of their towers,
And happy promises fulfill'd.

And I—perhaps if my intent
Could count on prediluvian age,
The labours I should then have spent
Might so attain their heritage,

But now before the pot can glow
With not to be discover'd gold,
At length the bellows shall not blow,
The furnace shall at last be cold.

Yet it is now too late to heal
The incapable and cumbrous shame
Which makes me when with men I deal
More powerless than the blind or lame.

No, I should love the city less
Even than this my thankless lore;
But I desire the wilderness
Or weeded landslips of the shore.

I walk my breezy belvedere
To watch the low or levant sun,
I see the city pigeons veer,
I mark the tower swallows run

Between the tower-top and the ground
Below me in the bearing air;
Then find in the horizon-round
One spot and hunger to be there.

And then I hate the most that lore
That holds no promise of success;
Then sweetest seems the houseless
    shore,
Then free and kind the wilderness.

Or ancient mounds that cover bones,
Or rocks where rockdoves do repair
And trees of terebinth and stones
And silence and a gulf of air.

There on a long and squarèd height
After the sunset I would lie,
And pierce the yellow waxen light
With free long looking, ere I die.

Let me be to Thee as the circling bird,
Or bat with tender and air-crisping wings
That shapes in half-light his departing
    rings,
From both of whom a changeless note is
    heard.

I have found my music in a common word,
Trying each pleasurable throat that sings
And every praisèd sequence of sweet
    strings,
And know infallibly which I preferred.

The authentic cadence was discovered late
Which ends those only strains that I
    approve,
And other science all gone out of date

And minor sweetness scarce made mention
of:
I have found the dominant of my range
and state—
Love, O my God, to call Thee Love and
Love.

Heaven-Haven

A nun takes the veil

I have desired to go
    Where springs not fail,
To fields where flies no sharp and
    sided hail
      And a few lilies blow.

And I have asked to be
    Where no storms come,
Where the green swell is in the havens
    dumb,
      And out of the swing of the sea.

The Habit of Perfection

✧

Elected Silence, sing to me
And beat upon my whorlèd ear,
Pipe me to pastures still and be
The music that I care to hear.

Shape nothing, lips; be lovely-dumb:
It is the shut, the curfew sent
From there where all surrenders come
Which only makes you eloquent.

Be shellèd, eyes, with double dark
And find the uncreated light:
This ruck and reel which you remark
Coils, keeps, and teases simple sight.

Palate, the hutch of tasty lust,
Desire not to be rinsed with wine:
The can must be so sweet, the crust
So fresh that come in fasts divine!

Nostrils, your careless breath that
    spend
Upon the stir and keep of pride,
What relish shall the censers send
Along the sanctuary side!

O feel-of-primrose hands, O feet
That want the yield of plushy sward,
But you shall walk the golden street
And you unhouse and house the Lord.

And, Poverty, be thou the bride
And now the marriage feast begun,
And lily-coloured clothes provide
Your spouse not laboured-at nor spun.

The Wreck of the Deutschland

❖

To the
happy memory of five Franciscan Nuns
exiles by the Falk Laws
drowned between midnight and morning of
Dec. 7th, 1875

PART THE FIRST

I

Thou mastering me
God! giver of breath and bread;
World's strand, sway of the sea;
Lord of living and dead;
Thou hast bound bones and veins in me,
fastened me flesh,

And after it almost unmade, what with
dread,
　　Thy doing: and dost thou touch me
　　afresh?
Over again I feel thy finger and find
thee.

2

　　I did say yes
　　O at lightning and lashed rod;
Thou heardst me truer than tongue
confess
　　Thy terror, O Christ, O God;
Thou knowest the walls, altar and hour
and night:
The swoon of a heart that the sweep
and the hurl of thee trod
　　Hard down with a horror of height:
And the midriff astrain with leaning of,
laced with fire of stress.

3

　　The frown of his face
　　Before me, the hurtle of hell

Behind, where, where was a, where was
    a place?
    I whirled out wings that spell
And fled with a fling of the heart to the
    heart of the Host.
My heart, but you were dovewinged, I
    can tell,
    Carrier-witted, I am bold to boast,
To flash from the flame to the flame
    then, tower from the grace to the
    grace.

4

    I am soft sift
    In an hourglass—at the wall
Fast, but mined with a motion, a
    drift,
    And it crowds and it combs to the
    fall;
I steady as a water in a well, to a poise,
    to a pane,
But roped with, always, all the way down
    from the tall

Fells or flanks of the voel, a vein
Of the gospel proffer, a pressure, a
    principle, Christ's gift.

5

    I kiss my hand
    To the stars, lovely-asunder
    Starlight, wafting him out of it; and
    Glow, glory in thunder;
Kiss my hand to the dappled-with-
    damson west:
Since, tho' he is under the world's
    splendour and wonder,
    His mystery must be instressed,
    stressed;
For I greet him the days I meet him, and
    bless when I understand.

6

    Not out of his bliss
    Springs the stress felt
    Nor first from heaven (and few know
    this)
    Swings the stroke dealt—

Stroke and a stress that stars and storms
    deliver,
That guilt is hushed by, hearts are
    flushed by and melt—
    But it rides time like riding a river
(And here the faithful waver, the
    faithless fable and miss.)

7

    It dates from day
    Of his going in Galilee;
    Warm-laid grave of a womb-life grey;
    Manger, maiden's knee;
The dense and the driven Passion, and
    frightful sweat;
Thence the discharge of it, there its
    swelling to be,
    Though felt before, though in high
    flood yet—
What none would have known of it,
    only the heart, being hard at bay,

Is out with it! Oh,
We lash with the best or worst
Word last! How a lush-kept plush-
capped sloe
Will, mouthed to flesh-burst,
Gush!—flush the man, the being with it,
sour or sweet,
Brim, in a flash, full!—Hither then, last
or first,
To hero of Calvary, Christ,'s feet—
Never ask if meaning it, wanting it,
warned of it—men go.

Be adored among men,
God, three-numberèd form;
Wring thy rebel, dogged in den,
Man's malice, with wrecking and
storm.
Beyond saying sweet, past telling of
tongue,

Thou art lightning and love, I found it,
  a winter and warm;
    Father and fondler of heart thou hast
      wrung:
Hast thy dark descending and most art
  merciful then.

10

  With an anvil-ding
    And with fire in him forge thy will
  Or rather, rather then, stealing as
    Spring
      Through him, melt him but master
        him still:
Whether at once, as once at a crash
  Paul,
Or as Austin, a lingering-out sweet skill,
  Make mercy in all of us, out of us all
Mastery, but be adored, but be adored
  King.

PART THE SECOND

11

'Some find me a sword; some
The flange and the rail; flame,
Fang, or flood' goes Death on drum,
And storms bugle his fame.
But wé dream we are rooted in earth—
Dust!
Flesh falls within sight of us, we, though
our flower the same,
Wave with the meadow, forget that
there must
The sour scythe cringe, and the blear
share come.

12

On Saturday sailed from
Bremen,
American-outward-bound,
Take settler and seamen, tell men with
women,
Two hundred souls in the round—

O Father, not under thy feathers nor
    ever as guessing
The goal was a shoal, of a fourth the
    doom to be drowned;
    Yet did the dark side of the bay of
      thy blessing
Not vault them, the millions of rounds
    of thy mercy not reeve even them in?

13

      Into the snows she sweeps,
    Hurling the haven behind,
    The Deutschland, on Sunday; and so
      the sky keeps,
    For the infinite air is unkind,
And the sea flint-flake, black-backed in
    the regular blow,
Sitting Eastnortheast, in cursed quarter,
    the wind;
    Wiry and white-fiery and whirlwind-
      swivellèd snow
Spins to the widow-making unchilding
    unfathering deeps.

14

She drove in the dark to
    leeward,
  She struck—not a reef or a rock
But the combs of a smother of sand:
    night drew her
  Dead to the Kentish Knock;
And she beat the bank down with her
    bows and the ride of her keel:
The breakers rolled on her beam with
    ruinous shock;
  And canvas and compass, the whorl
    and the wheel
Idle for ever to waft her or wind her
    with, these she endured.

15

Hope had grown grey hairs,
  Hope had mourning on,
Trenched with tears, carved with
    cares,
  Hope was twelve hours gone;

And frightful a nightfall folded rueful a
    day
Nor rescue, only rocket and lightship,
    shone,
    And lives at last were washing away:
To the shrouds they took,—they shook
    in the hurling and horrible airs.

16

        One stirred from the rigging
        to save
    The wild woman-kind below,
With a rope's end round the man,
    handy and brave—
    He was pitched to his death at a
    blow,
For all his dreadnought breast and braids
    of thew:
They could tell him for hours, dandled
    the to and fro
    Through the cobbled foam-fleece,
    what could he do

With the burl of the fountains of air,
  buck and the flood of the wave?

17

They fought with God's
  cold—
And they could not and fell to the
  deck
(Crushed them) or water (and
  drowned them) or rolled
With the sea-romp over the wreck.
Night roared, with the heart-break
  hearing a heart-broke rabble,
The woman's wailing, the crying of child
  without check—
Till a lioness arose breasting the
  babble,
A prophetess towered in the tumult, a
  virginal tongue told.

18

Ah, touched in your bower of
  bone

Are you! turned for an exquisite
    smart,
Have you! make words break from me
    here all alone,
    Do you!—mother of being in me,
        heart.
O unteachably after evil, but uttering
    truth,
Why, tears! is it? tears; such a melting, a
    madrigal start!
    Never-eldering revel and river of
        youth,
What can it be, this glee? the good you
    have there of your own?

19

    Sister, a sister calling
    A master, her master and mine!—
And the inboard seas run swirling and
    hawling;
    The rash smart sloggering brine
Blinds her; but she that weather sees one
    thing, one;

Has one fetch in her: she rears herself to
    divine
  Ears, and the call of the tall nun
To the men in the tops and the tackle
    rode over the storm's brawling.

20

  She was first of a five and
        came
  Of a coifèd sisterhood.
  (O Deutschland, double a desperate
    name!
  O world wide of its good!
But Gertrude, lily, and Luther, are two
    of a town,
Christ's lily and beast of the waste
    wood:
  From life's dawn it is drawn down,
Abel is Cain's brother and breasts they
    have sucked the same.)

21

  Loathed for a love men knew
      in them,

Banned by the land of their birth,
  Rhine refused them. Thames would
    ruin them;
    Surf, snow, river and earth
Gnashed: but thou art above, thou
    Orion of light;
Thy unchancelling poising palms were
    weighing the worth,
    Thou martyr-master: in thy sight
Storm flakes were scroll-leaved flowers,
    lily showers—sweet heaven was astrew
    in them.

22

    Five! the finding and sake
    And cipher of suffering Christ.
  Mark, the mark is of man's make
    And the word of it Sacrificed.
But he scores it in scarlet himself on his
    own bespoken,
Before-time-taken, dearest prizèd and
    priced—
    Stigma, signal, cinquefoil token

For lettering of the lamb's fleece,
  ruddying of the rose-flake.

23

  Joy fall to thee, father Francis,
  Drawn to the Life that died;
With the gnarls of the nails in thee,
  niche of the lance, his
  Lovescape crucified
And seal of his seraph-arrival! and these
  thy daughters
And five-livèd and leavèd favour and
  pride,
  Are sisterly sealed in wild waters,
To bathe in his fall-gold mercies, to
  breathe in his all-fire glances.

24

  Away in the loveable west,
  On a pastoral forehead of Wales,
I was under a roof here, I was at rest,
  And they the prey of the gales,
She to the black-about air, to the
  breaker, the thickly

Falling flakes, to the throng that catches
　　and quails
　　Was calling 'O Christ, Christ, come
　　　　quickly':
The cross to her she calls Christ to her,
　　christens her wild-worst Best.

25

　　　　The majesty! what did she
　　　　　　mean?
　　Breathe, arch and original Breath.
　　Is it love in her of the being as her
　　　　lover had been?
　　Breathe, body of lovely Death.
They were else-minded then, altogether,
　　the men
Woke thee with a *we are perishing* in the
　　weather of Gennesareth.
　　Or is it that she cried for the crown
　　　　then,
The keener to come at the comfort for
　　feeling the combating keen?

26

For how to the heart's
cheering
The down-dugged ground-hugged
grey
Hovers off, the jay-blue heavens
appearing
Of pied and peeled May!
Blue-beating and hoary-glow height; or
night, still higher,
With belled fire and the moth-soft
Milky Way,
What by your measure is the heaven
of desire,
The treasure never eyesight got, nor was
ever guessed what for the hearing?

27

No, but it was not these.
The jading and jar of the cart,
Time's tasking, it is fathers that
asking for ease

Of the sodden-with-its-sorrowing
        heart,
Not danger, electrical horror; then
    further it finds
The appealing of the Passion is tenderer
    in prayer apart:
        Other, I gather, in measure her mind's
Burden, in wind's burly and beat of
    endragonèd seas.

28

But how shall I . . . make
        me room there:
    Reach me a . . . Fancy, come
        faster—
Strike you the sight of it? look at it
    loom there,
        Thing that she . . . there then!
        the Master,
Ipse, the only one, Christ, King, Head:
He was to cure the extremity where he
    had cast her;
    Do, deal, lord it with living and dead;

Let him ride, her pride, in his triumph,
   despatch and have done with his
   doom there.

29

     Ah! there was a heart right!
   There was single eye!
Read the unshapeable shock night
   And knew the who and the why;
Wording it how but by him that present
   and past,
Heaven and earth are word of, worded
   by?—
   The Simon Peter of a soul! to the
   blast
Tarpeian-fast, but a blown beacon of
   light.

30

     Jesu, heart's light,
   Jesu, maid's son,
What was the feast followed the night
   Thou hadst glory of this nun?—
Feast of the one woman without stain.

For so conceivèd, so to conceive thee is
    done;
    But here was heart-throe, birth of a
      brain,
Word, that heard and kept thee and
    uttered thee outright.

31

      Well, she has thee for the
        pain, for the
    Patience; but pity of the rest of
      them!
Heart, go and bleed at a bitterer vein
    for the
    Comfortless unconfessed of
      them—
No not uncomforted: lovely-felicitous
    Providence
Finger of a tender of, O of a feathery
    delicacy, the breast of the
    Maiden could obey so, be a bell to,
      ring of it, and

Startle the poor sheep back! is the
    shipwrack then a harvest, does
    tempest carry the grain for thee?

32

    I admire thee, master of the
      tides,
  Of the Yore-flood, of the year's
    fall;
 The recurb and the recovery of the
  gulf's sides,
   The girth of it and the wharf of it
    and the wall;
Stanching, quenching ocean of a
  motionable mind;
Ground of being, and granite of it: past
 all
 Grasp God, throned behind
Death with a sovereignty that heeds but
 hides, bodes but abides;

33

    With a mercy that outrides
  The all of water, an ark

For the listener; for the lingerer with
  a love glides
    Lower than death and the dark;
A vein for the visiting of the past-prayer,
  pent in prison,
The-last-breath penitent spirits—the
  uttermost mark
    Our passion-plungèd giant risen,
The Christ of the Father compassionate,
  fetched in the storm of his strides.

34

    Now burn, new born to the
      world,
      Double-naturèd name,
    The heaven-flung, heart-fleshed,
      maiden-furled
        Miracle-in-Mary-of-flame,
Mid-numbered He in three of the
  thunder-throne!
Not a dooms-day dazzle in his coming
  nor dark as he came;
    Kind, but royally reclaiming his own;

A released shower, let flash to the shire,
    not a lightning of fire hard-hurled.

35

    Dame, at our door
    Drowned, and among our shoals,
Remember us in the roads, the
    heaven-haven of the Reward:
        Our King back, oh, upon English
        souls!
Let him easter in us, be a dayspring to
    the dimness of us, be a crimson-
    cresseted east,
More brightening her, rare-dear Britain,
    as his reign rolls,
        Pride, rose, prince, hero of us, high-
        priest,
Our hearts' charity's hearth's fire, our
    thoughts' chivalry's throng's Lord.

Penmaen Pool

❖

For the Visitors' Book at the Inn

Who long for rest, who look for pleasure
Away from counter, court, or school
O where live well your lease of leisure
But here at, here at Penmaen Pool?

You'll dare the Alp? you'll dart the skiff?
Each sport has here its tackle and tool:
Come, plant the staff by Cadair cliff;
Come, swing the sculls on Penmaen Pool.

What's yonder?—Grizzled Dyphwys dim:
The triple-hummocked Giant's Stool,
Hoar messmate, hobs and nobs with him
To halve the bowl of Penmaen Pool.

And all the landscape under survey,
At tranquil turns, by nature's rule,
Rides repeated topsyturvy
In frank, in fairy Penmaen Pool.

And Charles's Wain, the wondrous seven,
And sheep-flock clouds like worlds of
    wool,
For all they shine so, high in heaven,
Shew brighter shaken in Penmaen Pool.

The Mawddach, how she trips! though
    throttled
If floodtide teeming thrills her full,
And mazy sands all water-wattled
Waylay her at ebb, past Penmaen Pool.

But what's to see in stormy weather,
When grey showers gather and gusts are
    cool?
Why, raindrop-roundels looped together
That lace the face of Penmaen Pool.

Then even in weariest wintry hour
Of New Year's month or surly Yule
Furred snows, charged tuft above tuft,
    tower
From darksome darksome Penmaen Pool.

And ever, if bound here hardest home,
You've parlour-pastime left and (who'll
Not honour it?) ale like goldy foam
That frocks an oar in Penmaen Pool.

Then come who pine for peace or
    pleasure
Away from counter, court, or school,
Spend here your measure of time and
    treasure
And taste the treats of Penmaen Pool.

The Silver Jubilee

✧

*To James First Bishop of Shrewsbury
on the 25th Year of his Episcopate
July 28, 1876*

Though no high-hung bells or din
Of braggart bugles cry it in—
    What is sound? Nature's round
Makes the Silver Jubilee.

Five and twenty years have run
Since sacred fountains to the sun
    Sprang, that but now were shut,
Showering Silver Jubilee.

Feasts, when we shall fall asleep,
Shrewsbury may see others keep;
    None but you this her true,
This her Silver Jubilee.

Not today we need lament
Your wealth of life is some way spent:
    Toil has shed round your head
Silver but for Jubilee.

Then for her whose velvet vales
Should have pealed with welcome,
    Wales,
    Let the chime of a rhyme
Utter Silver Jubilee.

God's Grandeur

✦

The world is charged with the grandeur of
    God.
    It will flame out, like shining from
        shook foil;
    It gathers to a greatness, like the ooze of
        oil
Crushed. Why do men then now not reck
    his rod?
Generations have trod, have trod, have
    trod;
    And all is seared with trade; bleared,
        smeared with toil;
    And wears man's smudge and shares
        man's smell: the soil
Is bare now, nor can foot feel, being shod.

And for all this, nature is never spent;
   There lives the dearest freshness deep
      down things;
And though the last lights off the black
   West went
   Oh, morning, at the brown brink
      eastward, springs—
Because the Holy Ghost over the bent
   World broods with warm breast and
      with ah! bright wings.

The Starlight Night

❖

Look at the stars! look, look up at the
    skies!
      O look at all the fire-folk sitting in the
        air!
      The bright boroughs, the circle-citadels
        there!
Down in dim woods the diamond delves!
    the elves'-eyes!
The grey lawns cold where gold, where
    quickgold lies!
      Wind-beat whitebeam! airy abeles set
        on a flare!
      Flake-doves sent floating forth at a
        farmyard scare!
Ah well! it is all a purchase, all is a prize.

Buy then! bid then!—What?—Prayer,
   patience, alms, vows.
Look, look: a May-mess, like on orchard
   boughs!
      Look! March-bloom, like on mealed-
      with-yellow sallows!
These are indeed the barn; withindoors
   house
The shocks. This piece-bright paling shuts
   the spouse
      Christ home, Christ and his mother and
      all his hallows.

Spring

❖

Nothing is so beautiful as Spring—
   When weeds, in wheels, shoot long and
      lovely and lush;
   Thrush's eggs look little low heavens,
      and thrush
Through the echoing timber does so rinse
   and wring
The ear, it strikes like lightnings to hear
   him sing;
   The glassy peartree leaves and blooms,
      they brush
   The descending blue; that blue is all in a
      rush
With richness; the racing lambs too have
   fair their fling.

What is all this juice and all this joy?
  A strain of the earth's sweet being in the
    beginning
In Eden garden.——Have, get, before it cloy,
  Before it cloud, Christ, lord, and sour
    with sinning,
Innocent mind and Mayday in girl and
  boy,
  Most, O maid's child, thy choice and
    worthy the winning.

The Lantern Out of Doors

❖

Sometimes a lantern moves along the
    night,
    That interests our eyes. And who goes
        there?
    I think; where from and bound, I
        wonder, where,
With, all down darkness wide, his wading
    light?

Men go by me whom either beauty bright
    In mould or mind or what not else
        makes rare:
    They rain against our much-thick and
        marsh air

Rich beams, till death or distance buys
  them quite.

Death or distance soon consumes them:
  wind
    What most I may eye after, be in at the
      end
I cannot, and out of sight is out of mind.

Christ minds: Christ's interest, what to
  avow or amend
    There, éyes them, heart wánts, care
      haúnts, foot fóllows kínd,
Their ránsom, théir rescue, ánd first, fást,
  last friénd.

The Sea
and the Skylark

❖

On ear and ear two noises too old to end
   Trench—right, the tide that ramps
     against the shore;
    With a flood or a fall, low lull-off or all
     roar,
Frequenting there while moon shall wear
   and wend.

Left hand, off land, I hear the lark ascend,
   His rash-fresh re-winded new skeinèd
     score
    In crisps of curl off wild winch whirl,
     and pour

And pelt music, till none's to spill nor
     spend.

How these two shame this shallow and
     frail town!
     How ring right out our sordid turbid
          time,
Being pure! We, life's pride and cared-for
     crown,

     Have lost that cheer and charm of
          earth's past prime:
Our make and making break, are breaking,
     down
     To man's last dust, drain fast towards
          man's first slime.

The Windhover

To Christ our Lord

I caught this morning morning's minion,
   kingdom of daylight's dauphin, dapple-
   dawn-drawn Falcon, in his riding
     Of the rolling level underneath him
      steady air, and striding
High there, how he rung upon the rein of
   a wimpling wing
In his ecstasy! then off, off forth on swing,
   As a skate's heel sweeps smooth on a
     bow-bend: the hurl and gliding
     Rebuffed the big wind. My heart in
      hiding

Stirred for a bird,—the achieve of, the
  mastery of the thing!

Brute beauty and valour and act, oh, air,
    pride, plume, here
  Buckle! AND the fire that breaks from
    thee then, a billion
Times told lovelier, more dangerous, O my
  chevalier!

  No wonder of it: shéer plód makes
    plough down sillion
Shine, and blue-bleak embers, ah my dear,
  Fall, gall themselves, and gash gold-
    vermilion.

Pied Beauty

✤

Glory be to God for dappled things—
   For skies of couple-colour as a brinded
      cow;
      For rose-moles all in stipple upon
         trout that swim;
Fresh-firecoal chestnut-falls; finches' wings;
   Landscape plotted and pieced—fold,
      fallow, and plough;
      And áll trádes, their gear and tackle
         and trim.

All things counter, original, spare, strange;
   Whatever is fickle, freckled (who knows
      how?)
     With swift, slow; sweet, sour;
        adazzle, dim;
He fathers-forth whose beauty is past
   change:
       Praise him.

Hurrahing in Harvest

❖

Summer ends now; now, barbarous in
    beauty, the stooks arise
      Around; up above, what wind-walks!
        what lovely behaviour
      Of silk-sack clouds! has wilder, wilful-
        wavier
Meal-drift moulded ever and melted
    across skies?

I walk, I lift up, I lift up heart, eyes,
    Down all that glory in the heavens to
      glean our Saviour;
      And, éyes, heárt, what looks, what lips
        yet gave you a
Rapturous love's greeting of realer, of
    rounder replies?

And the azurous hung hills are his world-
  wielding shoulder
    Majestic—as a stallion stalwart, very-
      violet-sweet!—
These things, these things were here and
  but the beholder
    Wanting; which two when they once
      meet,
The heart rears wings bold and bolder
    And hurls for him, O half hurls earth
      for him off under his feet.

The Caged Skylark

❖

As a dare-gale skylark scanted in a dull
  cage
    Man's mounting spirit in his bone-
      house, mean house, dwells—
    That bird beyond the remembering his
      free fells;
This in drudgery, day-labouring-out life's
  age.

Though aloft on turf or perch or poor
  low stage,
    Both sing sometimes the sweetest,
      sweetest spells,
    Yet both droop deadly sómetimes in
      their cells

Or wring their barriers in bursts of fear or
  rage.

Not that the sweet-fowl, song-fowl, needs
  no rest—
Why, hear him, hear him babble and drop
  down to his nest,
  But his own nest, wild nest, no prison.

Man's spirit will be flesh-bound when
  found at best,
But uncumbered: meadow-down is not
  distressed
  For a rainbow footing it nor he for his
    bónes rísen.

In the Valley
of the Elwy

❖

I remember a house where all were good
  To me, God knows, deserving no such
    thing:
  Comforting smell breathed at very
    entering,
Fetched fresh, as I suppose, off some sweet
  wood.
That cordial air made those kind people a
  hood
  All over, as a bevy of eggs the mothering
    wing
  Will, or mild nights the new morsels of
    Spring:

Why, it seemed of course; seemed of right
   it should.

Lovely the woods, waters, meadows,
   combes, vales,
All the air things wear that build this
   world of Wales;
   Only the inmate does not correspond:
God, lover of souls, swaying considerate
   scales,
Complete thy creature dear O where it
   fails,
   Being mighty a master, being a father
      and fond.

The Loss
of the Eurydice

❖

Foundered March 24, 1878

The Eurydice—it concerned thee, O Lord:
Three hundred souls, O alas! on board,
    Some asleep unawakened, all un-
warned, eleven fathoms fallen

Where she foundered! One stroke
Felled and furled them, the hearts of oak!
    And flockbells off the aerial
Downs' forefalls beat to the burial.

For she did pride her, freighted fully, on
Bounden bales or a hoard of bullion?—

Precious passing measure,
Lads and men her lade and treasure.

She had come from a cruise, training
     seamen—
Men, boldboys soon to be men:
     Must it, worst weather,
Blast bole and bloom together?

No Atlantic squall overwrought her
Or rearing billow of the Biscay water:
     Home was hard at hand
And the blow bore from land.

And you were a liar, O blue March day.
Bright sun lanced fire in the heavenly bay;
     But what black Boreas wrecked her?
          he
Came equipped, deadly-electric,

A beetling baldbright cloud thorough
     England
Riding: there did storms not mingle? and
     Hailropes hustle and grind their

Heavengravel? wolfsnow, worlds of it, wind
   there?

Now Carisbrook keep goes under in gloom:
Now it overvaults Appledurcombe;
      Now near by Ventnor town
It hurls, hurls off Boniface Down.

Too proud, too proud, what a press she
   bore!
Royal, and all her royals wore.
      Sharp with her, shorten sail!
Too late; lost; gone with the gale.

This was that fell capsize.
As half she had righted and hoped to rise
      Death teeming in by her portholes
Raced down decks, round messes of
   mortals.

Then a lurch forward, frigate and men;
'All hands for themselves' the cry ran then;
      But she who had housed them thither

Was around them, bound them or wound
  them with her.

Marcus Hare, high her captain,
Kept to her—care-drowned and wrapped
  in
      Cheer's death, would follow
His charge through the champ-white water-
  in-a-wallow,

All under Channel to bury in a beach her
Cheeks: Right, rude of feature,
      He thought he heard say
'Her commander! and thou too, and thou
  this way.'

It is even seen, time's something server,
In mankind's medley a duty-swerver,
      At downright 'No or yes?'
Doffs all, drives full for righteousness.

Sydney Fletcher, Bristol-bred,
(Low lie his mates now on watery bed)

Takes to the seas and snows
As sheer down the ship goes.

Now her afterdraught gullies him too
   down;
Now he wrings for breath with the
   deathgush brown;
     Till a lifebelt and God's will
Lend him a lift from the sea-swill.

Now he shoots short up to the round air;
Now he gasps, now he gazes everywhere;
     But his eye no cliff, no coast or
Mark makes in the rivelling snowstorm.

Him, after an hour of wintry waves,
A schooner sights, with another, and saves,
     And he boards her in Oh! such joy
He has lost count what came next, poor
   boy,—

They say who saw one sea-corpse cold
He was all of lovely manly mould,

Every inch a tar,
Of the best we boast our sailors are.

Look, foot to forelock, how all things suit!
    he
Is strung by duty, is strained to beauty,
    And brown-as-dawning-skinned
With brine and shine and whirling wind.

O his nimble finger, his gnarled grip!
Leagues, leagues of seamanship
    Slumber in these forsaken
Bones, this sinew, and will not waken.

He was but one like thousands more,
Day and night I deplore
    My people and born own nation,
Fast foundering own generation.

I might let bygones be—our curse
Of ruinous shrine no hand or, worse,
    Robbery's hand is busy to
Dress, hoar-hallowèd shrines unvisited;

Only the breathing temple and fleet
Life, this wildworth blown so sweet,
  These daredeaths, ay this crew, in
Unchrist, all rolled in ruin—

Deeply surely I need to deplore it,
Wondering why my master bore it,
  The riving off that race
So at home, time was, to his truth and
 grace

That a starlight-wender of ours would say
The marvellous Milk was Walsingham Way
  And one—but let be, let be:
More, more than was will yet be.—

O well wept, mother have lost son;
Wept, wife; wept, sweetheart would be one:
  Though grief yield them no good
Yet shed what tears sad truelove should.

But to Christ lord of thunder
Crouch; lay knee by earth low under:

'Holiest, loveliest, bravest,
Save my hero, O Hero savest.

And the prayer thou hearst me making
Have, at the awful overtaking,
      Heard; have heard and granted
Grace that day grace was wanted.'

Not that hell knows redeeming,
But for souls sunk in seeming
      Fresh, till doomfire burn all,
Prayer shall fetch pity eternal.

The May Magnificat

May is Mary's month, and I
Muse at that and wonder why:
    Her feasts follow reason,
    Dated due to season—

Candlemas, Lady Day;
But the Lady Month, May,
    Why fasten that upon her,
    With a feasting in her honour?

Is it only its being brighter
Than the most are must delight her?
    Is it opportunest
    And flowers finds soonest?

Ask of her, the mighty mother:
Her reply puts this other
    Question: What is Spring?—
    Growth in every thing—

Flesh and fleece, fur and feather,
Grass and greenworld all together;
    Star-eyed strawberry-breasted
    Throstle above her nested

Cluster of bugle blue eggs thin
Forms and warms the life within;
    And bird and blossom swell
    In sod or sheath or shell.

All things rising, all things sizing
Mary sees, sympathising
    With that world of good,
    Nature's motherhood.

Their magnifying of each its kind
With delight calls to mind
    How she did in her stored
    Magnify the Lord.

Well but there was more than this:
Spring's universal bliss
    Much, had much to say
    To offering Mary May.

When drop-of-blood-and-foam-dapple
Bloom lights the orchard-apple
    And thicket and thorp are merry
    With silver-surfèd cherry.

And azuring-over greyball makes
Wood banks and brakes wash wet like
  lakes
    And magic cuckoocall
    Caps, clears, and clinches all—

This ecstasy all through mothering earth
Tells Mary her mirth till Christ's birth
    To remember and exultation
    In God who was her salvation.

Binsey Poplars

Felled 1879

My aspens dear, whose airy cages quelled,
Quelled or quenched in leaves the leaping
   sun,
All felled, felled, are all felled;
   Of a fresh and following folded rank
      Not spared, not one
      That dandled a sandalled
     Shadow that swam or sank
On meadow and river and wind-wandering
   weed-winding bank.

O if we but knew what we do
     When we delve or hew—
   Hack and rack the growing green!

Since country is so tender
To touch, her being só slender,
That, like this sleek and seeing ball
But a prick will make no eye at all,
Where we, even where we mean

     To mend her we end her,
   When we hew or delve:
After-comers cannot guess the beauty
  been.
Ten or twelve, only ten or twelve
   Strokes of havoc únselve
    The sweet especial scene,
  Rural scene, a rural scene,
  Sweet especial rural scene.

Duns Scotus's Oxford

❖

Towery city and branchy between towers;
Cuckoo-echoing, bell-swarmèd, lark-
    charmèd, rook-racked, river-rounded;
The dapple-eared lily below thee; that
    country and town did
Once encounter in, here coped and poisèd
    powers;

Thou hast a base and brickish skirt there,
    sours
That neighbour-nature thy grey beauty is
    grounded
Best in; graceless growth, thou hast
    confounded

Rural rural keeping—folk, flocks, and
  flowers.

Yet ah! this air I gather and I release
He lived on; these weeds and waters, these
  walls are what
He haunted who of all men most sways
  my spirits to peace;

Of realty the rarest-veinèd unraveller; a not
Rivalled insight, be rival Italy or Greece;
Who fired France for Mary without spot.

Henry Purcell

❖

The poet wishes well to the divine genius
of Purcell and praises him that,
whereas other musicians have given utterance
to the moods of man's mind, he has, beyond that,
uttered in notes the very make and
species of man as created both in him
and in all men generally.

Have fair fallen, O fair, fair have fallen, so
   dear
To me, so arch-especial a spirit as heaves in
   Henry Purcell,
An age is now since passed, since parted; with
   the reversal

Of the outward sentence low lays him,
   listed to a heresy, here.

Not mood in him nor meaning, proud fire
   or sacred fear,
Or love or pity or all that sweet notes not
   his might nursle:
It is the forgèd feature finds me; it is the
   rehearsal
Of own, of abrúpt sélf there so thrusts on,
   so throngs the ear.

Let him oh! with his air of angels then lift
   me, lay me! only I'll
Have an eye to the sakes of him, quaint
   moonmarks, to his pelted plumage
   under
Wings: so some great stormfowl, whenever
   he has walked his while

The thunder-purple seabeach plumèd
   purple-of-thunder,
If a wuthering of his palmy snow-pinions
   scatter a colossal smile
Off him, but meaning motion fans fresh
   our wits with wonder.

Peace

When will you ever, Peace, wild
   wooddove, shy wings shut,
Your round me roaming end, and under be
   my boughs?
When, when, Peace, will you, Peace? I'll
   not play hypocrite
To own my heart: I yield you do come
   sometimes; but
That piecemeal peace is poor peace. What
   pure peace allows
Alarms of wars, the daunting wars, the
   death of it?

O surely, reaving Peace, my Lord should
   leave in lieu

Some good! And so he does leave Patience
    exquisite,
That plumes to Peace thereafter. And when
    Peace here does house
He comes with work to do, he does not
    come to coo,
        He comes to brood and sit.

The Bugler's
First Communion

✦

A bugler boy from barrack (it is over the
   hill
There)—boy bugler, born, he tells me, of
   Irish
      Mother to an English sire (he
Shares their best gifts surely, fall how
   things will),

This very very day came down to us after a
   boon he on
My late being there begged of me,
   overflowing
      Boon in my bestowing,

Came, I say, this day to it—to a First
   Communion.

Here he knelt then ín regimental red.
Forth Christ from cupboard fetched, how
   fain I of feet
        To his youngster take his treat!
Low latched in leaf light housel his too
   huge godhead.

There! and your sweetest sendings, ah
   divine,
By it, heavens, befall him! as a heart
   Christ's darling, dauntless;
        Tongue true, vaunt- and tauntless;
Breathing bloom of a chastity in mansex
   fine.

Frowning and forefending angel-warder
Squander the hell-rook ranks sally to
   molest him;
        March, kind comrade, abreast him;

Dress his days to a dexterous and starlight
  order.

How it dóes my heart good, visiting at that
  bleak hill,
When limber liquid youth, that to all I
  teach
          Yields tender as a pushed peach,
Hies headstrong to its wellbeing of a self-
  wise self-will!

Then though I should tread tufts of
  consolation
Dáys áfter, só I in a sort deserve to
          And do serve God to serve to
Just such slips of soldiery Christ's royal
  ration.

Nothing élse is like it, no, not all so
  strains
Us: fresh youth fretted in a bloomfall all
  portending
          That sweet's sweeter ending;

Realm both Christ is heir to and thére
  réigns.

O now well work that sealing sacred
  ointment!
O for now charms, arms, what bans off
  bad
        And locks love ever in a lad!
Let mé though see no more of him, and
  not disappointment

Those sweet hopes quell whose least me
  quickenings lift,
In scarlet or somewhere of some day seeing
      That brow and bead of being,
An our day's God's own Galahad. Though
  this child's drift

Seems by a divíne doom chánnelled, nor do
  I cry
Disaster there; but may he not rankle and
  roam

In backwheels though bound
home?——
That left to the Lord of the Eucharist, I
here lie by;

Recorded only, I have put my lips on pleas
Would brandle adamantine heaven with
ride and jar, did
Prayer go disregarded:
Forward-like, but however, and like
favourable heaven heard these.

Morning Midday and Evening Sacrifice

❖

The dappled die-away
Cheek and wimpled lip,
The gold-wisp, the airy-grey
Eye, all in fellowship—
This, all this beauty blooming,
This, all this freshness fuming,
Give God while worth consuming.

Both thought and thew now bolder
And told by Nature: Tower;
Head, heart, hand, heel, and shoulder
That beat and breathe in power—
This pride of prime's enjoyment

Take as for tool, not toy meant
And hold at Christ's employment.

The vault and scope and schooling
And mastery in the mind,
In silk-ash kept from cooling,
And ripest under rind—
What life half lifts the latch of,
What hell stalks towards the snatch
    of,
Your offering, with despatch, of!

Andromeda

Now Time's Andromeda on this rock
  rude,
With not her either beauty's equal or
Her injury's, looks off by both horns of
  shore,
Her flower, her piece of being, doomed
  dragon food.
  Time past she has been attempted and
    pursued
By many blows and banes; but now hears
  roar
A wilder beast from West than all were,
  more
Rife in her wrongs, more lawless, and
  more lewd.

Her Perseus linger and leave her tó her
    extremes?—
Pillowy air he treads a time and hangs
His thoughts on her, forsaken that she
    seems,
    All while her patience, morselled into
        pangs,
Mounts; then to alight disarming, no one
    dreams,
With Gorgon's gear and barebill / thongs
    and fangs.

The Candle Indoors

Some candle clear burns somewhere I
   come by.
I muse at how its being puts blissful back
With yellowy moisture mild night's blear-
   all black,
Or to-fro tender trambeams truckle at the
   eye.
By that window what task what fingers ply,
I plod wondering, a-wanting, just for lack
Of answer the eagerer a-wanting Jessy or
   Jack
There God to aggrándise, God to
   glorify.—

Come you indoors, come home; your
   fading fire

Mend first and vital candle in close heart's
    vault:
You there are master, do your own desire;
What hinders? Are you beam-blind, yet to
    a fault
In a neighbour deft-handed? are you that
    liar
And, cast by conscience out, spendsavour
    salt?

The Handsome Heart

❖

At a Gracious Answer

'But tell me, child, your choice; what shall
   I buy
You?'—'Father, what you buy me I like
   best.'
With the sweetest air that said, still plied
   and pressed,
He swung to his first poised purport of
   reply.

What the heart is! which, like carriers let
   fly—
Doff darkness, homing nature knows the
   rest—

To its own fine function, wild and self-
   instressed,
Falls light as ten years long taught how to
   and why.

Mannerly-hearted! more than handsome
   face—
Beauty's bearing or muse of mounting
   vein,
All, in this case, bathed in high hallowing
   grace . . .

Of heaven what boon to buy you, boy, or
   gain
Not granted!—Only . . . O on that path
   you pace
Run all your race, O brace sterner that
   strain!

At the Wedding March

✦

God with honour hang your head,
Groom, and grace you, bride, your
  bed
With lissome scions, sweet scions,
Out of hallowed bodies bred.

Each be other's comfort kind:
Déep, déeper than divined,
Divine charity, dear charity,
Fast you ever, fast bind.

Then let the March tread our ears:
I to him turn with tears
Who to wedlock, his wonder wedlock,
Déals tríumph and immortal years.

Felix Randal

❖

Felix Randal the farrier, O he is dead
    then? my duty all ended,
Who have watched his mould of man, big-
    boned and hardy-handsome
Pining, pining, till time when reason
    rambled in it and some
Fatal four disorders, fleshed there, all
    contended?

Sickness broke him. Impatient he cursed at
    first, but mended
Being anointed and all; though a heavenlier
    heart began some
Months earlier, since I had our sweet
    reprieve and ransom

Tendered to him. Ah well, God rest him all
    road ever he offended!

This seeing the sick endears them to us, us
    too it endears.
My tongue had taught thee comfort, touch
    had quenched thy tears,
Thy tears that touched my heart, child,
    Felix, poor Felix Randal;

How far from then forethought of, all thy
    more boisterous years,
When thou at the random grim forge,
    powerful amidst peers,
Didst fettle for the great grey drayhorse his
    bright and battering sandal!

Brothers

How lovely the elder brother's
Life all laced in the other's,
Lóve-laced!—what once I well
Witnessed; so fortune fell.
When Shrovetide, two years gone,
Our boys' plays brought on
Part was picked for John,
Young Jóhn; then fear, then joy
Ran revel in the elder boy.
Their night was come now; all
Our company thronged the hall;
Henry, by the wall,
Beckoned me beside him;
I came where called, and eyed him
By meanwhiles; making mý play

Turn most on tender byplay.
For, wrung all on love's rack,
My lad, and lost in Jack,
Smiled, blushed, and bit his lip;
Or drove, with a diver's dip,
Clutched hands down through
     clasped knees—
Truth's tokens tricks like these,
Old tell tales, with what stress
He hung on the imp's success.
Now the other was bráss-bóld:
Hé had no work to hold
His heart up at the strain;
Nay, roguish ran the vein.
Two tedious acts were past;
Jack's call and cue at last;
When Henry, heart-forsook,
Dropped eyes and dared not look.
Eh, how áll rúng!
Young dog, he did give tongue!
But Harry—in his hands he has flung
His tear-tricked cheeks of flame

For fond love and for shame.
    Ah Nature, framed in fault,
There's comfort then, there's salt;
Nature, bad, base, and blind,
Dearly thou canst be kind;
There dearly thén, deárly,
I'll cry thou canst be kind.

Spring and Fall

To a young child

Márgarét, are you gríeving
Over Goldengrove unleaving?
Leáves, líke the things of man, you
With your fresh thoughts care for, can
  you?
Áh! ás the heart grows older
It will come to such sights colder
By and by, nor spare a sigh
Though worlds of wanwood leafmeal lie;
And yet you wíll weep and know why.
Now no matter, child, the name:

Sórrow's spríngs áre the same.
Nor mouth had, no nor mind, expressed
What heart heard of, ghost guessed:
It ís the blight man was born for,
It is Margaret you mourn for.

Inversnaid

This darksome burn, horseback brown,
His rollrock highroad roaring down,
In coop and in comb the fleece of his foam
Flutes and low to the lake falls home.

A windpuff-bonnet of fáwn-fróth
Turns and twindles over the broth
Of a pool so pitchblack, féll-frówning,
It rounds and rounds Despair to drowning.

Degged with dew, dappled with dew
Are the groins of the braes that the brook
  treads through,
Wiry heathpacks, flitches of fern,
And the beadbonny ash that sits over the
  burn.

What would the world be, once bereft
Of wet and of wilderness? Let them be
    left,
O let them be left, wildness and wet;
Long live the weeds and the wilderness yet.

As kingfishers catch fire, dragonflies dráw
fláme;
As tumbled over rim in roundy wells
Stones ring; like each tucked string tells,
each hung bell's
Bow swung finds tongue to fling out broad
its name;
Each mortal thing does one thing and the
same:
Deals out that being indoors each one
dwells;
Selves—goes itself; *myself* it speaks and
spells;
Crying *Whát I dó is me: for that I came.*

Í say móre: the just man justices;
Kéeps gráce: thát keeps all his goings
　　graces;
Acts in God's eye what in God's eye he
　　is—
Chríst—for Christ plays in ten thousand
　　places,
Lovely in limbs, and lovely in eyes not his
To the Father through the features of
　　men's faces.

Ribblesdale

Earth, sweet Earth, sweet landscape, with
  leavès throng
And louchèd low grass, heaven that dost
  appeal
To, with no tongue to plead, no heart to
  feel;
That canst but only be, but dost that
  long—

Thou canst but be, but that thou well
  dost; strong
Thy plea with him who dealt, nay does
  now deal,
Thy lovely dale down thus and thus bids
  reel

Thy river, and o'er gives all to rack or
  wrong.

And what is Earth's eye, tongue, or heart
  else, where
Else, but in dear and dogged man?—Ah,
  the heir
To his own selfbent so bound, so tied to
  his turn,
To thriftless reave both our rich round
  world bare
And none reck of world after, this bids
  wear
Earth brows of such care, care and dear
  concern.

The Leaden Echo
and the Golden Echo

❖

(Maidens' song from St. Winefred's Well)

THE LEADEN ECHO

How to kéep—is there ány any, is there
    none such, nowhere known some, bow or
    brooch or braid or brace, láce, latch or
    catch or key to keep
Back beauty, keep it, beauty, beauty,
    beauty, . . . from vanishing away?
Ó is there no frowning of these wrinkles,
    rankèd wrinkles deep,
Dówn? no waving off of these most

mournful messengers, still messengers,
  sad and stealing messengers of grey?
No there's none, there's none, O no there's
  none,
Nor can you long be, what you now are,
  called fair,
Do what you may do, what, do what you
  may,
And wisdom is early to despair:
Be beginning; since, no, nothing can be
  done
To keep at bay
Age and age's evils, hoar hair,
Ruck and wrinkle, drooping, dying, death's
  worst, winding sheets, tombs and worms
  and tumbling to decay;
So be beginning, be beginning to despair.
O there's none; no no no there's none:
Be beginning to despair, to despair,
Despair, despair, despair, despair.

Spare!
There ís one, yes I have one (Hush there!);
Only not within seeing of the sun,
Not within the singeing of the strong sun,
Tall sun's tingeing, or treacherous the
    tainting of the earth's air,
Somewhere elsewhere there is ah well
    where! one,
Ońe. Yes I cán tell such a key, I dó know
    such a place,
Where whatever's prized and passes of us,
    everything that's fresh and fast flying of
    us, seems to us sweet of us and swiftly
    away with, done away with, undone,
Undone, done with, soon done with, and
    yet dearly and danger-ously sweet
Of us, the wimpled-water-dimpled, not-by-
    morning-matchèd face,

The flower of beauty, fleece of beauty, too
   too apt to, ah! to fleet,
Never fleets móre, fastened with the
   tenderest truth
To its own best being and its loveliness of
   youth: it is an ever-lastingness of, O it is
   an all youth!
Come then, your ways and airs and looks,
   locks, maiden gear, gallantry and gaiety
   and grace,
Winning ways, airs innocent, maiden
   manners, sweet looks, loose locks, long
   locks, lovelocks, gaygear, going gallant,
   girl-grace—
Resign them, sign them, seal them, send
   them, motion them with breath,
And with sighs soaring, soaring síghs
   deliver
Them; beauty-in-the-ghost, deliver it, early
   now, long before death

Give beauty back, beauty, beauty, beauty,
  back to God, beauty's self and beauty's
  giver.
See; not a hair is, not an eyelash, not the
  least lash lost; every hair
Is, hair of the head, numbered.
Nay, what we had lighthanded left in surly
  the mere mould
Will have waked and have waxed and have
  walked with the wind what while we
  slept,
This side, that side hurling a heavyheaded
  hundredfold
What while we, while we slumbered.
O then, weary then whý should we tread?
  O why are we so haggard at the heart, so
  care-coiled, care-killed, so fagged, so
  fashed, so cogged, so cumbered.
When the thing we freely fórfeit is kept
  with fonder a care,
Fonder a care kept than we could have kept
  it, kept

Far with fonder a care (and we, we should
   have lost it) finer, fonder
A care kept.—Where kept? Do but tell us
   where kept, where.—
Yonder.—What high as that! We follow,
   now we follow.—Yonder, yes yonder,
   yonder,
Yonder.

The Blessed Virgin Compared to the Air We Breathe

Wild air, world-mothering air,
Nestling me everywhere,
That each eyelash or hair
Girdles; goes home betwixt
The fleeciest, frailest-flixed
Snowflake; that's fairly mixed
With, riddles, and is rife
In every least thing's life;
This needful, never spent,
And nursing element;
My more than meat and drink,
My meal at every wink;

This air, which, by life's law,
My lung must draw and draw
Now but to breathe its praise,
Minds me in many ways
Of her who not only
Gave God's infinity
Dwindled to infancy
Welcome in womb and breast,
Birth, milk, and all the rest
But mothers each new grace
That does now reach our race—
Mary Immaculate,
Merely a woman, yet
Whose presence, power is
Great as no goddess's
Was deemèd, dreamèd; who
This one work has to do—
Let all God's glory through,
God's glory which would go
Through her and from her flow
Off, and no way but so.
　　　I say that we are wound

With mercy round and round
As if with air: the same
Is Mary, more by name.
She, wild web, wondrous robe,
Mantles the guilty globe,
Since God has let dispense
Her prayers his providence:
Nay, more than almoner,
The sweet alms' self is her
And men are meant to share
Her life as life does air.

　　If I have understood,
She holds high motherhood
Towards all our ghostly good
And plays in grace her part
About man's beating heart,
Laying, like air's fine flood,
The deathdance in his blood;
Yet no part but what will
Be Christ our Saviour still.
Of her flesh he took flesh:
He does take fresh and fresh,

Though much the mystery how,
Not flesh but spirit now
And makes, O marvellous!
New Nazareths in us,
Where she shall yet conceive
Him, morning, noon, and eve;
New Bethlems, and he born
There, evening, noon, and morn—
Bethlem or Nazareth,
Men here may draw like breath
More Christ and baffle death;
Who, born so, comes to be
New self and nobler me
In each one and each one
More makes, when all is done,
Both God's and Mary's Son.

    Again, look overhead
How air is azurèd;
O how! nay do but stand
Where you can lift your hand
Skywards: rich, rich it laps
Round the four fingergaps.

Yet such a sapphire-shot,
Charged, steepèd sky will not
Stain light. Yea, mark you this:
It does no prejudice.
The glass-blue days are those
When every colour glows,
Each shape and shadow shows.
Blue be it: this blue heaven
The seven or seven times seven
Hued sunbeam will transmit
Perfect, not alter it.
Or if there does some soft,
On things aloof, aloft,
Bloom breathe, that one breath
    more
Earth is the fairer for.
Whereas did air not make
This bath of blue and slake
His fire, the sun would shake,
A blear and blinding ball
With blackness bound, and all
The thick stars round him roll

Flashing like flecks of coal,
Quartz-fret, or sparks of salt,
In grimy vasty vault.

So God was god of old:
A mother came to mould
Those limbs like ours which are
What must make our daystar
Much dearer to mankind;
Whose glory bare would blind
Or less would win man's mind.
Through her we may see him
Made sweeter, not made dim,
And her hand leaves his light
Sifted to suit our sight.

Be thou then, O thou dear
Mother, my atmosphere;
My happier world, wherein
To wend and meet no sin;
Above me, round me lie
Fronting my froward eye
With sweet and scarless sky;
Stir in my ears, speak there

Of God's love, O live air,
Of patience, penance, prayer:
World-mothering air, air wild,
Wound with thee, in thee isled,
Fold home, fast fold thy child.

To What Serves Mortal Beauty?

❖

To what serves mortal beauty | —
    dangerous; does set dancing blood—the
    O-seal-that-so | feature, flung prouder
    form
Than Purcell tune lets tread to? | See: it
    does this: keeps warm
Men's wits to the things that are; | what
    good means—where a glance
Master more may than gaze, | gaze out of
    countenance.
Those lovely lads once, wet-fresh |
    windfalls of war's storm,

How then should Gregory, a father, | have
    gleanèd else from swarm-
ed Rome? But God to a nation | dealt that
    day's dear chance.
    To man, that needs would worship |
        block or barren stone,
Our law says: Love what are | love's
    worthiest, were all known;
World's loveliest—men's selves. Self |
    flashes off frame and face.
What do then? how meet beauty? | Merely
    meet it; own,
Home at heart, heaven's sweet gift; | then
    leave, let that alone.
Yea, wish that though, wish all, | God's
    better beauty, grace.

Spelt from Sibyl's Leaves

❖

Earnest, earthless, equal, attuneable, |
    vaulty, voluminous, . . . stupendous
Evening strains to be tíme's vást, | womb-
    of-all, home-of-all, hearse-of-all night.
Her fond yellow hornlight wound to the
    west, | her wild hollow hoarlight hung
    to the height
Waste; her earliest stars, earl-stars, | stárs
    principal, overbend us,
Fíre-féaturing heaven. For earth | her being
    has unbound, her dapple is at an end, as-
tray or aswarm, all throughther, in throngs;
    | self ín self steepèd and páshed—qúite

Disremembering, dísmémbering | áll now.
    Heart, you round me right
With: Óur évening is over us; óur night |
    whélms, whélms, ánd will end us.
Only the beak-leaved boughs dragonish |
    damask the tool-smooth bleak light;
    black,
Ever so black on it. Óur tale, O óur oracle!
    | Lét life, wáned, ah lét life wind
Off hér once skéined stained véined varíety
    | upon, áll on twó spools; párt, pen,
    páck
Now her áll in twó flocks, twó folds—
    black, white; | right, wrong; reckon but,
    reck but, mind
But thése two; wáre of a wórld where bút
    these | twó tell, each off the óther; of a
    rack
Where, selfwrung, selfstrung, sheathe-and
    shelterless, | thóughts agáinst thoughts
    ín groans grínd.

(The Soldier)

❖

Yes. Whý do we áll, seeing of a soldier,
   bless him? bless
Our redcoats, our tars? Both these being,
   the greater part,
But frail clay, nay but foul clay. Here it
   is: the heart,
Since, proud, it calls the calling manly,
   gives a guess
That, hopes that, makesbelieve, the men
   must be no less;
It fancies, feigns, deems, dears the artist
   after his art;
And fain will find as sterling all as all is
   smart,

And scarlet wear the spirit of wár thére
   express.

Mark Christ our King. He knows war,
   served this soldiering through;
He of all can reeve a rope best. There he
   bides in bliss
Now, and séeing somewhére some mán
   do all that man can do,
For love he leans forth, needs his neck
   must fall on, kiss,
And cry 'O Christ-done deed! So God-
   made-flesh does too:
Were I come o'er again' cries Christ 'it
   should be this'.

(Carrion Comfort)

❖

Not, I'll not, carrion comfort, Despair, not
   feast on thee;
Not untwist—slack they may be—these
   last strands of man
In me ór, most weary, cry *I can no more*. I
   can;
Can something, hope, wish day come, not
   choose not to be.
But ah, but O thou terrible, why wouldst
   thou rude on me
Thy wring-world right foot rock? lay a
   lionlimb against me? scan
With darksome devouring eyes my bruisèd
   bones? and fan,

O in turns of tempest, me heaped there;
  me frantic to avoid thee and flee?

  Why? That my chaff might fly; my grain
    lie, sheer and clear.
Nay in all that toil, that coil, since (seems)
  I kissed the rod,
Hand rather, my heart lo! lapped strength,
  stole joy, would laugh, chéer.
Cheer whom though? the hero whose
  heaven-handling flung me, fóot tród
Me? or me that fought him? O which one?
  is it each one? That night, that year
Of now done darkness I wretch lay
  wrestling with (my God!) my God.

No worst, there is none. Pitched past pitch
   of grief,
More pangs will, schooled at forepangs,
   wilder wring.
Comforter, where, where is your
   comforting?
Mary, mother of us, where is your relief?
My cries heave, herds-long; huddle in a
   main, a chief
Woe, world-sorrow; on an age-old anvil
   wince and sing—
Then lull, then leave off. Fury had shrieked
   'No ling-
ering! Let me be fell: force I must be
   brief'.

O the mind, mind has mountains; cliffs
  of fall
Frightful, sheer, no-man-fathomed. Hold
  them cheap
May who ne'er hung there. Nor does long
  our small
Durance deal with that steep or deep.
  Here! creep,
Wretch, under a comfort serves in a
  whirlwind: all
Life death does end and each day dies with
  sleep.

To seem the stranger lies my lot, my life
Among strangers. Father and mother dear,
Brothers and sisters are in Christ not near
And he my peace my parting, sword and
   strife.

  England, whose honour O all my heart
    woos, wife
To my creating thought, would neither
   hear
Me, were I pleading, plead nor do I: I
   wear-
y of idle a being but by where wars are rife.

  I am in Ireland now; now I am at a
    third
Remove. Not but in all removes I can

Kind love both give and get. Only what
    word
Wisest my heart breeds dark heaven's
    baffling ban
Bars or hell's spell thwarts. This to hoard
    unheard,
Heard unheeded, leaves me a lonely began.

I wake and feel the fell of dark, not day.
What hours, O what black hoürs we have
    spent
This night! what sights you, heart, saw;
    ways you went!
And more must, in yet longer light's delay.
    With witness I speak this. But where I
      say
Hours I mean years, mean life. And my
    lament
Is cries countless, cries like dead letters
    sent
To dearest him that lives alas! away.

I am gall, I am heartburn. God's most
   deep decree
Bitter would have me taste: my taste was
   me;
Bones built in me, flesh filled, blood
   brimmed the curse.
   Selfyeast of spirit a dull dough sours. I
      see
The lost are like this, and their scourge to
   be
As I am mine, their sweating selves; but
   worse.

Patience, hard thing! the hard thing but to
  pray,
But bid for, Patience is! Patience who asks
Wants war, wants wounds; weary his times,
  his tasks;
To do without, take tosses, and obey.
  Rare patience roots in these, and, these
    away,
Nowhere. Natural heart's ivy, Patience
  masks
Our ruins of wrecked past purpose. There
  she basks
Purple eyes and seas of liquid leaves all
  day.

We hear our hearts grate on themselves: it kills
   To bruise them dearer. Yet the rebellious wills
Of us we do bid God bend to him even so.
   And where is he who more and more distils
Delicious kindness?—He is patient. Patience fills
His crisp combs, and that comes those ways we know.

My own heart let me more have pity on;
    let
Me live to my sad self hereafter kind,
Charitable; not live this tormented mind
With this tormented mind tormenting yet.
    I cast for comfort I can no more get
By groping round my comfortless, than
    blind
Eyes in their dark can day or thirst can
    find
Thirst's all-in-all in all a world of wet.

Soul, self; come, poor Jackself, I do advise
You, jaded, let be; call off thoughts awhile
Elsewhere; leave comfort root-room; let
    joy size

At God knows when to God knows what;
  whose smile
's not wrung, see you; unforeseen times
  rather—as skies
Betweenpie mountains—lights a lovely
  mile.

Tom's Garland

Upon the Unemployed

Tom—garlanded with squat and surly steel
Tom; then Tom's fallowbootfellow piles
    pick
By him and rips out rockfire homeforth—
    sturdy Dick;
Tom Heart-at-ease, Tom Navvy: he is all
    for his meal
Sure, 's bed now. Low be it: lustily he his
    low lot (feel
That ne'er need hunger, Tom; Tom seldom
    sick,
Seldomer heartsore; that treads through,
    prickproof, thick

Thousands of thorns, thoughts) swings
   though. Commonweal
Little I reck ho! lacklevel in, if all had
   bread:
What! Country is honour enough in all us
   —lordly head,
With heaven's lights high hung round, or,
   mother-ground
That mammocks, mighty foot. But nó way
   sped,
Nor mind nor mainstrength; gold go
   garlanded
With, perilous, O nó; nor yet plod safe
   shod sound;
              Undenizened, beyond bound
Of earth's glory, earth's ease, all; no one,
   nowhere,
In wide the world's weal; rare gold, bold
   steel, bare

In both; care, but share
care—
This, by Despair, bred Hangdog dull; by
Rage,
Manwolf, worse; and their packs infest the
age.

Harry Ploughman

❖

Hard as hurdle arms, with a broth of
   goldish flue
Breathed round; the rack of ribs; the
   scooped flank; lank
Rope-over thigh; knee-nave; and barrelled
   shank—
         Head and foot, shoulder and
   shank—

By a grey eye's heed steered well, one crew,
   fall to;
Stand at stress. Each limb's barrowy brawn,
   his thew
That onewhere curded, onewhere sucked or
   sank—
         Soared or sank—,

Though as a beechbole firm, finds his, as
   at a roll-call, rank
And features, in flesh, what deed he each
   must do—
         His sinew-service where do.

He leans to it, Harry bends, look. Back,
   elbow, and liquid waist
In him, all quail to the wallowing o' the
   plough: 's cheek crim-sons; curls
Wag or crossbridle, in a wind lifted,
   windlaced—
         See his wind-lilylocks-laced;
Churlsgrace, too, child of Amansstrength,
   how it hangs or hurls
Them—broad in bluff hide his frowning
   feet lashed! raced
With, along them, cragiron under and cold
   furls—
         With-a-fountain's shining-shot
   furls.

That Nature Is a Heraclitean Fire and of the Comfort of the Resurrection

Cloud-puffball, torn tufts, tossed pillows |
   flaunt forth, then chevy on an air-
built thoroughfare: heaven-roysterers, in
   gay-gangs | they throng; they glitter in
   marches.
Down roughcast, down dazzling whitewash,
   | wherever an elm arches,
Shivelights and shadowtackle in long |
   lashes lace, lance, and pair.
Delightfully the bright wind boisterous |
   ropes, wrestles, beats earth bare

Of yestertempest's creases; | in pool and
  rut peel parches
Squandering ooze to squeezed | dough,
  crust, dust; stanches, starches
Squadroned masks and manmarks | treadmire toil there
Footfretted in it. Million-fuelèd, | nature's
  bonfire burns on.
But quench her bonniest, dearest | to her,
  her clearest-selvèd spark
Man, how fast his firedint, | his mark on
  mind, is gone!
Both are in an unfathomable, all is in an
  enormous dark
Drowned. O pity and indig | nation!
  Manshape, that shone
Sheer off, disseveral, a star, | death blots
  black out; nor mark
        Is any of him at all so stark
But vastness blurs and time | beats level.
  Enough! the Resurrec-tion,

A heart's-clarion! Away grief's gasping, | joyless days, dejection.
                    Across my foundering deck shone
A beacon, an eternal beam. | Flesh fade, and mortal trash
Fall to the residuary worm; | world's wildfire, leave but ash:
                    In a flash, at a trumpet crash,
I am all at once what Christ is, | since he was what I am, and
This Jack, joke, poor potsherd, | patch, matchwood, immortal diamond,
                    Is immortal diamond.

In honour of

St. Alphonsus Rodriguez

❖

Laybrother of the Society of Jesus

Honour is flashed off exploit, so we say;
And those strokes once that gashed flesh
  or galled shield
Should tongue that time now, trumpet
  now that field,
And, on the fighter, forge his glorious day.
On Christ they do and on the martyr may;
But be the war within, the brand we wield
Unseen, the heroic breast not outward-
  steeled,

Earth hears no hurtle then from fiercest
    fray.

    Yet God (that hews mountain and
        continent,
Earth, all, out; who, with trickling
    increment,
Veins violets and tall trees makes more and
    more)
Could crowd career with conquest while
    there went
Those years and years by of world without
    event
That in Majorca Alfonso watched the
    door.

Justus quidem tu es, Domine, si disputem tecum:
verumtamen justa loquar ad te:
Quare via impiorum prosperatur? &c.

Thou art indeed just, Lord, if I contend
With thee; but, sir, so what I plead is just.
Why do sinners' ways prosper? and why
    must
Disappointment all I endeavour end?
    Wert thou my enemy, O thou my friend,
How wouldst thou worse, I wonder, than
    thou dost
Defeat, thwart me? Oh, the sots and thralls
    of lust
Do in spare hours more thrive than I that
    spend,

Sir, life upon thy cause. See, banks and
  brakes
Now, leavèd how thick! lacèd they are
  again
With fretty chervil, look, and fresh wind
  shakes
Them; birds build—but not I build; no,
  but strain,
Time's eunuch, and not breed one work
  that wakes.
Mine, O thou lord of life, send my roots
  rain.

The shepherd's brow, fronting forked
    lightning, owns
The horror and the havoc and the glory
Of it. Angels fall, they are towers, from
    heaven—a story
Of just, majestical, and giant groans.
But man—we, scaffold of score brittle
    bones;
Who breathe, from groundlong babyhood
    to hoary
Age gasp; whose breath is our *memento
    mori*—
What bass is *our* viol for tragic tones?
He! Hand to mouth he lives, and voids
    with shame;
And, blazoned in however bold the name,

Man Jack the man is, just; his mate a
   hussy.
And I that die these deaths, that feed this
   flame,
That . . . in smooth spoons spy life's
   masque mirrored: tame
My tempests there, my fire and fever
   fussy.

To R.B.

The fine delight that fathers thought; the
    strong
Spur, live and lancing like the blowpipe
    flame,
Breathes once and, quenchèd faster than it
    came,
Leaves yet the mind a mother of immortal
    song.
Nine months she then, nay years, nine
    years she long
Within her wears, bears, cares and combs
    the same:
The widow of an insight lost she lives,
    with aim

Now known and hand at work now never
   wrong.
   Sweet fire the sire of muse, my soul
      needs this:
I want the one rapture of an inspiration.
O then if in my lagging lines you miss
The roll, the rise, the carol, the creation,
My winter world, that scarcely breathes
   that bliss
Now, yields you, with some sighs, our
   explanation.